In Search of Cuba

In Search of Cuba

Richard M. Grove

SandCrab Books

Published by
SandCrab Books
www.hiddenbrookpress.com

Copyright © 2020 Hidden Brook Press
Copyright © 2020 Richard M. Grove

All rights for writing revert to the author. All rights for book, layout and design remain with Hidden Brook Press. No part of this book may be reproduced except by a reviewer who may quote brief passages in a review. The use of any part of this publication reproduced, transmitted in any form or by any means, electronic, mechanical, photocopied, recorded or otherwise stored in a retrieval system without prior written consent of the publisher is an infringement of the copyright law.

In Search of Cuba
by Richard M. Grove

Layout and Design – Richard M. Grove
Cover Design – Richard M. Grove
Cover Photograph – Richard M. Grove
B/W Photographs – Richard M. Grove

Printed and bound in USA
Typeset in Garamond

Library and Archives Canada Cataloguing in Publication

Title: In search of Cuba / Richard M. Grove.
Other titles: Poems. Selections (2020)
Names: Grove, Richard M. (Richard Marvin), 1953 - author.
    | Container of (work): Grove, Richard M. (Richard Marvin), 1953 - View of contrasts.
    | Container of (work): Grove, Richard M. (Richard Marvin), 1953 - Trip to Banis, Cuba.
Description: Poems.
Identifiers: Canadiana (print) 2020030237X
    | Canadiana (ebook) 20200303112
    | ISBN 9781989786093 (softcover)
    | ISBN 9781989786086 (ebook)
Subjects: LCSH: Cuba—Poetry.
Classification: LCC PS8563.R75 A6 2020
    | DDC C811/.54—dc23

Table of Content

Book 1
A View of Contrasts – *p. 1*

Book 2
A Trip to Banis, Cuba – *p. 49*

Author Bio – *p. 84*

Book 1

A View of Contrasts

This book was first published in 2002 by
EBIP
ISBN – 1-894553-02-0

*This book is dedicated
to my dear wife, Kim,
and our friends,
Bill and Juli,
who adventured to Cuba
with us.*

*Much gratitude
is extended
to Kim,
who has stood by me
in so many ways,
in life, in my writing
and the continuous adventures of life
that took us to Cuba.*

Bill and Julie

Richard (Tai) and Kim

Cuba Here We Come
1999

4:30am, not even dawn
November 26th takes us
in misty obscurity to the
Toronto Pearson Airport.
Limo cruises the calm,
almost serene stillness
of barren 401
with four fidgeting friends,
grinning, with wide-eyed
anticipation.

Luggage stowed in trunk with
snorkels, swim suites and suntan oil,
thick books and cameras.
Passports clutched in one hand
tickets and reservations
clenched in other with
dreams and hopes
of sun, sand and snoozes.

Leave Home Without It

When we arrived
in Cuban luxury
our tour guide announced
with wide eyed smile,
Visa and MasterCard are welcome
but leave your American Express
at home.

Hard to Believe We are in Cuba

Salt-laden drips ran
from my hair, down
my cheek to my lips.
I woke from my sun-worshipping
dream state to the sudden salty
reminder that I was on a soft,
tan, sandy beach in Cuba

I was no longer in my Toronto condo bed
being lured by computer, email,
time restraints and the bottom line.

The cool, turquoise ocean,
paces away, stirred by westerly winds
beckoning me with disbelief
is my relaxing reality
at least for a week.

More

In the middle of November,
everything is sweeter,
better in Cuba than in Toronto.

The steamed milk for my morning coffee
is more rich.

The blossom kissing afternoon sun
shines more brightly.

The palm shimmering breeze
of early evening is more alluring.

Orion's midnight belt
sparkles more clearly.

In the middle of November,
everything is sweeter,
better in Cuba than in Toronto.

Mango Juice and Coffee Every Morning

StarBucks and Second Cup,
you are a sham put to shame.
Go to the Atlantic shore
of the southern coast of Cuba
and learn how to make real coffee.
Its full-bodied, smooth flavour
with a slight under bite of calm, bitter
swirls in the mouth
after being caressed by the dew of mango.
It is enough to bring any slumbering soul
into the expectation
of what adventures might lie
beyond the horizon of noon.

Could I Ever Get My Fill of Cuban Mango Juice

On our first day in Cuba with our lunch
of pescado*
followed by tropical fruit
I had my first real glass of
ice-cold mango juice.
While, yes,
I have had this golden delight
at home in Toronto
but it could hardly be compared.
Lifeless and pale and a bit too sweet
was my experience at home
but here under the Cuban morning sky
with a dancing heart
it is like drinking glasses of sweetened
sunlight mixed with a dash of gratitude.
Here, sipped at pool's edge,
before an afternoon siesta,
under grass umbrellas,
serenaded by hopping Cuban sparrows
it is like drinking the gentle
cream of life

lightly stirred with the longing for more.
Here, nurcing this glass of golden nectar
before or after a second Pina-Colada
in evening's gentle breeze
it's like drinking a velvet caress.
Could one ever get enough
Cuban mango juice.

pescado – fish

A Cuban Sun Shower

Lush, outstretched palm fronds,
sweep the Cuban sky,
gently fanning salt air
as if to wave away
the single cloud
that grins overhead
christening our morning
with a sun shower
of expectation.

Undampened Spirits

Bill,
our resident climatologist
and meteorological kind of guy
dashes to the window
for invigorating gaze
peering past dancing palm leaves
presses forehead to glass
once again excited by yet another
deluge of warm rain
that will last
only as long as a
Cuban tropical moment.

Shimmying and Bowing

Early one evening a hurricane
dashed through our resort.
.05 on the hurricane scale.
The fact is it was no more
than a pelting flash
but for us tourists
it was a drenching thrill.
It flailed at us horizontally
from every direction
for 3/4 of an hour at most.
It wiped the palm trees
into a Latin frenzied dance.
Palm fronds flung
from side to side,
shimmying and bowing
to each other
in jerking frantic motion
protecting our balcony
from reaching rain.

As quickly as it was born
it died a sudden death
leaving us ample opportunity
to stroll the ravaged
palm strewn beach
to ponder the now
Cuban star lit sky.

An Early Morning Walk

I was the first to amble onto the beach
for an early morning walk that morning.
6:20 am footprints pressed deep
into salt laden sand
tossed by rough seas
the night before.
A warm foaming crest licking my heels
as I was drawn down past the sailboats
and kayaks resting in drifts of still wet sand.
Their chattering stays,
clicked out a Cuban song of stiff wind.
My walk took me north
past time-swept tree roots
and wind-beaten stumps of ancient palms.
I continued at brisk pace
down past cairns of raked seaweed
stacked by beach workers the day before.
I walked still further north
past the Eagle Bay Scuba Shop
where, with curtains drawn,
there was no evidence of this day's
eager tourists that will soon converge
for diving lessons.

Still further north
with the Atlantic beating the shore on my right
I stooped combing the sands
for penny size, alabaster white shells
securing them one by one in my pocket
for later inspection
when I would reveal my cherished collection
to anyone that finds beach trinkets of interest.
Still further north
my walk came to a predicted halt
at black lava cliffs
placed there ten millennium ago,
when mother earth was still being born.
Beaten by thousands upon thousands of years
these jagged faces
whisper to me that my witnessing
is not even a millisecond
in the story of wind and sea.

Coral Protrusions
Lure Investigation

There were these two fellows
shall I call them Bill and Tai?
They went for a kayaking adventure
in the thrashing ocean off the Atlantic coast
of Cuba one day.
They headed out flailing dipping paddles
without a care.
Full of brash confidence
and a longing for happenstance
or an impetuous tempted incident.

This pursuance of adventure
proceeded as expected,
gentle waves hardly demanded
our bow entry advance
as we proceeded further
from sunworshipper's beach.
Undulating fingers of emerald seaweed
waved us on as we skimmed
crystal clear water.
Distant coral protrusions lured investigation.

Two miles out into the ocean
out of sight from beach
on roaring foam edge
stood thrashings
that beaconed abandonment.

Bow piercing wash of foam thrilled
these two Canadian city dwellers.
Salt foam stings eyes as waves cascade over-head,
beating shoulders.
Heart throbbing rushes
pulse through us like javelins on coursing crest
over exposed jagged coral.
Success demands another
Bow crashing attempt.
Time after time we shoot
the thrilling gauntlet of eventuality,
past the mouth of hazard
till we were not willing to tempt
fate one more time with incident.
Fully satiated with adventure
we were beckoned back to the luxury

of toweled-sun-tanning turf,
our rash pursuance
took us safely through
boyish rite of passage.

From the Heart
of Strumming Cuban Performers

"Kiss me as if it is the last time you will ever kiss me."
rolled over Cuban red lipped strumming senoritas

"Hold me like it is our last night on earth together."
spilled over tented lunch in Santiago de Cuba

"Do you know I love you like no other."
Jet black hair cascaded over white, cotton laced shoulders

"You are the only love I will ever have."
Nimble fingers strum black guitar.

"Mi amour, Mi amour, you are the only one for me."
Velvet voices pour Caribbean song into the air
"Kiss me as if it is the last time you will ever kiss me."

**I Only Have Eyes For You My Love
Though I Must Confess
My Middle Aged Fantasy**

I only have eyes for you, my love,
though I must confess
I more than glanced
at a pretty Cuban head turner
while you were not looking.

I only have eyes for you, my love,
though I must confess
the copper tone buxom senorita,
licked by the Caribbean sun,
caressed by the Cuban breeze,
winked longingly at me.

I only have eyes for you, my love,
though I must confess
that she had a smile for me
that grew as I strolled closer.
She nodded at me and held out her hand
as if to invite me to dance.

I only have eyes for you, my love,
though I must confess
what she said to me
as I drew close enough to touch.
"Where have you been?" she said
"You have been gone for such a long time."
as she was greeted a Pina-Colada
placed in her hand
by her 22-year-old muscular,
bronze toy boy,
blond, with tattooed pecs
that made me blush,
cower, pretending
that I had not noticed
the freckle on her inner thigh.
Sucking in my stomach I walked
with deliberation
mirroring her blind
lack of acknowledgment.

I only have eyes for you, my love
though I must confess.

They May Be on the Bus to Havana For All We Know

Where are the girls?
We turned our heads for only a moment
to surreptitiously surrender a glance
at a slender, firm, oiled,
topless sun-worshipper
for an innocent millisecond glare,
as discreetly as one could
and still get a decent look.
In that very, very short short moment,
our pretty Canadian senoritas were gone.
Maybe our stride was broken
for longer than a male ego moment.
With quickened pace
we dart to catch up with Kim and Juli.

A Trypdich Woven
Around A Single Cuban Cigar

1 The Smoking Room

Amellio, a stout black-haired, friendly Cuban
graciously sells me a fat stoggy.
Invitingly he points me towards
the somewhat darkened
cedar panelled smoking room
decorated with man's false pride of dominance,
animal collaged hides hang in picture scenes
beside cigar box labels framed
in dark wooden opulence.
Free standing trophy size ashtrays pose
beside squeaky
man size cowhide sofa and juxtaposed arm chairs.
A coffee table stands at foot resting height
encouraging a reclined position
and the inclination to
"puff".

Don't sit down here
if you are not intending to light up
a cigar with me
for this is a "smoking" room
Not a room for the faint of constitution
or slight of breath.
This is not a room to relax and read a good book,
chat or even to write a poem for that matter.
It is inextricably a smoking room
where taking long ponderous
incisive puffs of a Cuban cigar
is the sole reason for being.

2 The Smoke Ring

The ease of blowing smoke rings
came back to me like riding a bicycle
both learned in adolescence.
Once you know how, you never forget.
It is like dragging black silk
across your bare arm.
The warm smoke roles
sensuously off your tongue
and through your "O" pierced lips.

Precisely pinch the hefty cigar
between forefinger and thumb.
Caulk your head slightly to one side
and take a long even drag.
Blow halting billows with
contemplative precision.
Smoke ring satisfaction
will shimmy down your spine.

3 The Aftermath

Some exercises of ponderance and ritual
are not worth partaking.
What a wretched, revolting habit
some men partake in.
To think that I would ever again
stick a wad of burning rolled up tobacco
between my lips and puff.
A substance that not even a worm
with any common sense
would even crawl upon.
Why would I light up
this putrid, acidic, dry, brown leaf
and voluntarily take a puff and then,
with arrogance, later lean wantingly
to kiss my lovely wife.

While I cannot promise in full faith
that I will never in my life time
smoke another cigar
it is though likely that I will
only in fading memory
imbibe in this retched ritual again.

Now let me retreat to my hotel room
brush my teeth, shower, wash my hair
and go through the ritualistic exorcism
of rinsing the vial scent from my
inner and outer being.

Sunday November 27th 1999
Dear Barry:
Straight to Hell in a Hand Basket

We have been relaxing under
the southern sun of Cuba for two days now.
Snorkelling, ocean kayaking,
swimming with the dolphins,
long walks on tan beach,
writing time each morning,
bus ride to see the Cuban country-side
and now a Cuban cigar
smoked in the hotel cedar panelled
smoking room
while relaxing in a squeaky leather sofa
with a lime and rum
ice chilled drink.

Well, straight to hell in a hand basket
do not stop at "Go" to collect $200.
If you would like to join me in hell
I will mail you a cigar.
It will be waiting for you in Edmonton
when you get back

from your Caribbean sailing adventure.
I know you are somewhere south
in these climes.

I met a fellow called John
in the cigar store.
I will forever remember him,
affectionately,
as the friendly tattooed ,
nipple-pierced,
tongue-pierced,
man from Ireland
with whom I shared a puff of my cigar
and accepted his personal endorsement
of my mild selection.

This ceremonial puff is dedicated to you, Barry,
and our many memories that rattle in time.
I toast to you, Barry, in absentia
I toast the notion of vastness of experience
that makes the spice of life.
I smoke this now wretched weed
down to the finger-burning nub

as a ceremonial salute to your willingness to
take the plunge of adventure that many,
maybe most,
are not brave enough to partake in.
I toast tattooed John, the Irishman,
and his double, belly-buttoned, pierced partner
as a salute to individuality.
I wish you were here
to clink an icy glass with me
as a salute to future unborn adventures.

Guadalavaca to Santiago de Cuba

40 minutes in the air from
Guadalavaca to Santiago De Cuba
250 Kilometres per hour escaping
any reminiscence of Toronto.
500 to 600 metres above emerald flowing
untamed jungle,
peering out doorless cabin
of our time-ravaged helicopter
a tired old Russian war machine transformed
into tourist convenience for sight seers
parallels ancient volcanic mountains
softened, tempered by time.

Helicopter Trip to Santiago de Cuba

The tops of palm trees zipped by
in the plummeting distance,
ocean languored on the breezeless horizon.
With white knuckles we clung
to our polished wooden bench,
no seatbelt.
A slender, braded, blue silk rope, trembled,
whipping across the open door.
Twelve of us pink tourists vibrate in dread
as we roared our way to Santiago de Cub
in our Aerogaviota Airline, Russian helicopter.
We thundered
towards the Sierra Maestra Mountain, serrated,
skyline.
Our tour guide kissed the ground and crossed himself
as soon as we landed –
"Dear Lord, let me see my family one more time."

A Guide Through History With New Cuban Friend Ra L Santos L Pez From Holguin

Revolution Square
We passed further through history with
Che Guevara, the Castro brothers,
General Mancada, Bastista, Ridas, Monroy
in air-conditioned minivan.
Too hot to get out.

We are reminded of Fidel
with Che, at right hand.
liberators of the people
11 million benefactors
embrace new leader.

We are told about
the Cuban legacy of courage
based on the spirit of
the Father of the Fatherland
Carlos Manuel de Cespedes
author, poet, lawyer freed his slaves
and declared Cuban independence

37

Castillo San Pedro de la Roca
(*Castle Saint Peter of the Rock*)

St. Peter the Apostle, disciple of Jesus Christ,
the faith of the Spaniards
who built this fortified monument of protection,
a garrison never overthrown, divinely protected,
were well justified in naming the fort
after their faith in you,
now a tourist snapshot attraction for millions
gazing south, out of sight to Jamaica
your foundation, thick walls and parapets
still stand strong. Your concrete gunwales
never yielding.

In the cool dark recesses
of your now empty arsenal
where not even spiders live is a woman
strapping on her pregnant belly.
Her compañera's begging shift is finished.
It is now time for her to parade
the prenatal protrusion.
"Por favor. Para mi hijo por nacer por favor."
Please. For my unborn child, please.
A few pesos please. Unos pesos por favor.

Cementerio Chorro De Maita
Eutierro 25 en exhibicion
25 on display at archeological site.

No special dispensation
for these twenty-five
long-dead natives on display.
Newly unearthed by archeologists
now forever remembered by bones.
Skulls placed like ivory trinkets
on stone pillows.
Time burnished bones
in motionless nightmare
posing for gawking tourists.
Empty socket grimaces
staring in direction of beckoning sea
brought out of rest to pose in
perpetual state of melancholy.
Satirical skeletal grins
never to rest again.

Castle El Maro

1640
Castle El Maro
the oldest Spanish fort
having never been plundered
by any hostile force.
A defensive bastion
firmly perched 100 metres
above ever-pitching
emerald Caribbean Sea.
Time painted ancient walls with
pock-marked stains of history,
the signifiers of
endurance and persistence.
View to Jamaica is pointed to
past silver horizon,
out of sight
over cold stone turrets
beyond ancient lava out-cropping's
pounded and beaten,
worn by the millennium.

Enshrined

Che Guevera

You have been reduced
to a pop icon
hand in hand with Mickey Mouse
you stroll the aisles of
capitalism and commerce.

It took only 30 short years
after you were martyred
for your face to be enshrined
on Bill's and my Christmas present,
a $16.95, electronic,
battery operated,
plastic, wrist watch
worn with pride as a symbol of
our Canadian freedom
to roam freely
on Cuban soil
with US dollars.

A View of Contrasts

Taxi trip into distant Cuban mountains
takes us to a lament of dry red clay
with palm rimmed horizons
surrounded by lush jungle homogeny.
Lush banana plantations fill
gently rolling valleys past
concrete, tin-capped, peasant huts.
Cactus hedgerows protect
modest, laboured gardens from
roving speckled pigs and
white bearded Billy goats.

Tame adventures end, taxi takes us back
to North American style opulence called
creature comforts of pressed linen,
steamed milk and chilled Pina-Coladas.
Home, past roadside open wells where
post siesta farmers water their
rib-clad burros,
sending us on our way with gentle
smiling waves of naiveté.

Capitulation

A beggarly, wrinkled face of an old woman
is pressed wantingly to the cool glass
of our luxurious mini-van.
Her eyes grip me tight.
I turn away
directing my gaze to the other side of the road.
If this was my grandmother I would weep.
I would give her the shirt off my back
but a stranger with no teeth, outstretch hand
quivering, mumbling in Spanish.

We thought that we were protected,
sheltered from the heat, pollution and poverty
of Santiago de Cuba
as we sat there with our tour guide
sharing our afternoon's experience.

With clawing persistence
she bustles to the other side of the van
where I attempt to shoo her away
the way one would an annoying fly,
a begging dog but she is persistent
in her relentless quest for a peso.

I capitulate to her endurance
she is rewarded
with a single US dollar bill
passed out into the heat
through a slender opening
I make in the window.

In the end her persistence pays off
she gets what she wants
in valued spendable cash
only so I can get what I want,
peace from groping want.
A small price for solitude.
I shrink into myself and wish
I had given her ten
or a hundred or a hug or or or.

"I Am Here to Serve You and Partake of Your Charity."

Feral cats befriend dallying sun-drenched tourists
flirting with softness and big black eyes of yearning
they mew their trained beckonings.
"Pity me for I am unfed and unloved by anyone
other than you. I am here to serve you
and partake of your charity.
I exist because of you and for you.
If you give of yourself you will feel better
and I will feel better for having served.
Can I get you a coffee sir?
Another and yet another free Pina-Colada
more food or simply a bigger smile.
Can I make your bed for you sir,
and expect nothing but a one dollar tip in return.
What you give me for my generous services
will feed my children and unborn child for a week.
Pity me for I am unfed and unloved by anyone
other than you. I am here to serve you
and partake of your charity.
We are both sides of the same coin called
Give and Take,
Be sure your give equals your take"

Book 2

A Trip to Banes, Cuba, 2002

This book was first published in 2008 by
HBP
ISBN – 978-1-897475-20-1

to opening one's eyes

Preface

My wife, Kim, and I have travelled to Cuba many times and have fallen in love with the people, the cultural differences and the landscape. We have made many life-long friends and visit as often as we can afford. In our early years of travelling in Cuba, we mostly stayed in beach-side resorts that isolated us from the daily lives and living conditions of most Cubans.

Trips like this day trip to Banes in 2002 were an eye opener to the poverty and drudgery that many Cubans lived. Since then we have travelled from the music and culture-filled heart of downtown Havana to the poorest dirt patch, tin roof areas that one can reach only in a four-wheel-drive jeep then further still by oxen cart. We have seen lush plantations, gorgeous waterfalls and ravines. We have seen dry red earth plots of land that sustain little more than scrub bush and a scrawny goat but we keep going back. Why? Because there is something that is more real than the earth and warm breeze. It is the people, the warm hearted people.

Since writing this short collection of poems I have learned to know Cuba much better and have learned to see past, or through, or between the poverty to the inner joy of the people. Their lives are often simple, poor in materialism but abundant in spiritual richness. In my imagination some parts of this land harken back to a simple low-tech farm life style of the 1920's. Despite the poverty there is joy; despite the poverty there is life and hope. Yes, many may be poor, even dirt poor, in respect to things they own. However, since writing this collection over six years ago, I have learned to see beyond poverty to the wealth of knowledge these people possess about what is important in life.

The irony in publishing this collection is that when I first wrote these poems I sadly thought that my eyes had been opened to the real Cuba. I was shocked and deeply disturbed to see the poverty that affected the young and the old, the dogs and the horses, the houses and the potholed thoroughfares. Now after many years of travelling and living there for a month or two at a time, my eyes are opened further and I see much more. Yes there are still many skinny dogs and horses, there are still houses that are dilapidated and some with roofs blown off and not replaced but I have learned to see the pride in the people and recognize that, for the most part, the poverty is a reflection of little resources rather than lethargy, laziness or sloth. The hope, the fortitude, the ingenuity, the spirit, the heart of the people is what helps them to survive and do the best with what they have.

I feel that the poems in this short collection are still worth publishing but they need to be read from the perspective of a naive, blind tourist that could not see the true heart of the people that live and work there.

Why do we keep going back to Cuba? Because we are constantly and joyfully surprised by what lies behind the poverty in the souls of the people.

i

Nowhere in Banes,
absolutely nowhere,
that I could see,
as we passed through,
is there even a single
square inch of prosperity
let alone opulence
or even the slightest
sign of wealth.

For me, the tourist,
US dollars brimming visitor
eyes wide open
mind closed with judgment
concealed smugly
tight to chest
I stroll unaware of my perspective.
Every where we turned
literally in every direction
we see poverty

rippling into the street
dripping over dusty curb
into dusty gutters
winding through
dusty social degradation.

Maybe,
many, many years ago
houses had been painted but
so many years ago
that colour has faded
so many years ago
that all luster
all pride
seems to have vanished
bleach by a merciless sun.
Has all joy
dimmed into shadowy past?

ii

Produce for sale
from front stoops.
One small cabbage offered
by a hovering shrinking
old lady, toothless.
Ten radishes
held out, offered with one hand
by dirty-face child
begging with the other
trading for a smile.
A small bunch of onions,
a single string of braided garlic.
Rice for sale by a burly man
on an old bicycle,
a bent wheel.
Always very little
selling hope for a few centavos.

iii

Stinking old cars and trucks
ancient,
pumping, spewing exhaust,
dodging bicycles and carts
drawn by weary old
droop-necked horses.
Have they ever been brushed
groomed with love?
So skinny I wonder
have they lived
merely on polluted Banes air
all their lives.

iv

Small dogs
as scrawny as the horses
barking, begging
scraps thrown
quiet, content
at least for a moment.

V

Skinny chicken tethered
a one foot radius
dictated by scrap of twine
as scrawny as the dog
as scrawny as the horse
as scrawny as the hope
that wilts in late evening
dust, clucking, scratching
barren earth
no lush grass to peck in.
Scraps, no grain thrown,
more clucking,
soon to be some ones
scrawny dinner.
No fat will float on her broth.

vi

Catholic cathedral
obviously poor
faces dusty desolate city square.

Fidel was married here.
When?
No one seems to remember.
How old is the church?
No one seems to remember.
Clean and kept with reverence
there is no sense of capitalizing
on Castro notoriety here.
No donation box
front and centre.
No post cards for sale.
No old lady begging or
pregnant mother selling despair.
Just poverty.
Clean poverty
scrubbed with love.

Outside the church – no luster
not even lust beams
from dead eyes.
Though everyone is busy
going
coming
people mingle
in lifeless groups.
Merging as a colourless
grey painting.

vii

A cat,
a dirty old skinny cat
darts
across street over puddle
under fence of bound twigs
and rusty scraps of tin,
flattened.
There is no purr left in this cat.
The cat is as scrawny as the dogs
as scrawny as the chicken
as scrawny as the horses
but still there is life.

viii

I noticed
there were no garbage cans.
In fact no garbage, no waist
everything is used,
every scrap,
so poor there is nothing
to through away,
no waist,
no garbage
no garbage cans.

ix

Guilt,
uncomfortable guilt trails us
shadowing every turn we take.
Our cab driver is content
to wait as long as he must
as we languor in the streets
taking pictures of want
before returning us to
five star smoked salmon
lobster tails
and service with a smile.

The longer we keep him waiting
the more we will pay in guilt
the bigger the tip.
It is getting dark
and our guilt has grown
to a fair size ball and chain
that we drag up one street
and down the next.

We want to give
to relieve the guilt
but there is no product to buy
no service to consume
no one to tip.

A very few pesos
tinkle to the palm
of an old lady
clink into the cup
of the one-legged man
wearing a pink flip flop
that neither flips
nor flop.
Where is the other?

X

We are only half way to hunger
but finally we look for a place
to have dinner.
Finally we can leave
some money in the city.
Wency, our Cuban friend and guide
shows us to a "private" restaurant.
Restauranta Roberto.
The only "safe" place to eat
he announces.
"I would not trust
you to the other restaurants."
Down another dusty street
past a scrawny dog
to a pair of saloon doors
that squeak as we timidly
push our way in.

xi

Roberto,
a fine, smiling Cuban man
greets us with a handshake
as the swinging doors
slap us in the back.
Binvienido, Welcome!
His smile is twice as wide
as the three table restaurant.
This proudly converted garage,
concrete floor, cracked,
is clean but obviously aged
and not like good wine.
The plastic,
flowered table-cloth screams
blue and pink.
The undecorated varnished masonite
wall panels reflect
the glare of a naked
circular fluorescent bulb
hanging

unceremoniously dangles, blinking
from bare wires
from the middle
of the oil stained ceiling.
With tentative stride we are seated.
Pulling our paper napkin,
half each,
carefully over our judgment
we sit with thirsty anticipation.

xii

A menu was proudly presented
as sparse as it was,
fried lamb,
        fried pork,
                fried chicken.
Skinny chicken at best I thought.
Dare I trust the pork?
I will have lamb.
Salad - no lettuce
tomatoes,
        cucumbers,
                shredded cabbage
presented as an elaborate gift.
Beans and rice,
        fried banana,
and "smashed" banana.

It was all delicious.

The bill arrived
for the three of us.
We were shocked at 175 pesos.
So much for so little I thought.
Conversion to under $7.00 plus a tip
was a relief.
Paying with a smile
      we were finally guilt free.
10 USA dollars buys a lot of freedom.

xiii

The power went out during dinner.
Candles were quickly lit
though blown out
as soon as electricity resumed.
No ceremony of romance
was allowed to linger.
The cost of candles
was impetus for conservation.
Pleasantries continued
in bright light of bare bulb
small talk dwindled.
Our enjoyable
Banes "private" restaurant experience
came to an end.
Mucho gracias señora.
I privately hoped never to return.

xiv

Did every spark
of life in Banes
revolve around this
one little garage restaurant?
We stepped back through
flapping doors
back to our haunting
perception of poverty.
Everywhere we turned
lack reared its head.
Were we blind?
Did the tourist cocoon
that we drifted in on
distort our perception
and show us nothing
but the commodity called need?

XV

I would have called him a beggar
if at home in Toronto,
a street person at best
but maybe only old and stooped,
plodding.
He walked passed us
close and slow
enough that we bumped into him
as we laughed our way into the street.
He didn't even look up
from where he was going.
No time to offer an apology
or a peso.

xvi

We wander through the dark
back to the cab
past a dilapidated house
we passed earlier,
don't sneeze it will fall over.
It has not yet slipped off of its
precarious stilts
into garbage glutted gully.

Back home this would be
prime real estate
filled with groomed grass and flowers,
looking down into a lush ravine.
The front door still locked
as if someone will soon arrive from work.
Shutters closed.
"Closed for the season." they said
as if a modern Muskoka cottage.
"Back in the spring."
but no one will return to this house.

No one will come to repair
the collapsing roof
or fix the sagging footings.
It will inevitably fall
further, furthere down the hill,
into the ruin of poverty,
irrecoverable poverty.

xvii

On the corner
under a tall shade tree
stands a derelict house.
Listing
like the other into gully,
now nothing
more than raw materials,
salvage.
Wood strips,
with care could be pried
from the past, ripped
from history to build anew.
Might I have gone in the dark
if I were Cuban
with shame tucked out of site
to steel what could be
my misplaced fortune?
Was it honesty
that prevented its pilfer?

xviii

Cab doors slam
driver starts the engine
with eager fingers.
The gush of air conditioning
cranked to high
greeting our demands.
On our way out of the city
we dodge pot holes,
a broken palm branch
and yes a skinny cat.

People, tired
stroll home from work,
a hard day serving us or our kind.
Some of them
may have served us at breakfast
and some might still serve us
before we leave.
We do not recognize them
but that is from a lack
of looking beyond our wants.

In the bright lights of breakfast
they do not look poor
but we see no faces.
With Pina Colada out stretched
there is no sense of poverty.
Serving us at pool side
or making our beds
there seems no lack.
There smile seems genuine
and full of life
as they receive their tips
that will carry them
just far enough
back to poverty.

Richard M. Grove, otherwise known to friends as Tai, divides his time between a condo in Toronto and a house in Brighton. The Brighton house is in Presqu'ile Provincial Park, half way between Toronto and Kingston where he and his wife Kim run a B&B. He is a Poet, Prose Writer, Publisher, Photographer, Painter, Graphic Designer and is the Poet Laureate of Brighton. He is the founding president of the CCLA – Canada Cuba Literary Alliance. You can find his Cuba Blog at http://cubablog.hiddenbrookpress.com/.

Including this book he has 20 titles to his name and his images have been used in many books as well as on the cover of almost 75 books. His writer's blog can be found at: https://richardgrovewriter.wordpress.com/.

In 2020 he was the founder of "The Poetry Pandemic Project" that reached poets and readers around the world. He is the Editor-in-chief of "Devour: Art & Lit Canada". He has had over 100 poems and essays published in periodicals around the world as well as having been published in over 30 anthologies. You can find his publishing company at: www.HiddenBrookPress.com.

His art and photographs are in over 30 corporate collections across Canada. He graduated from Ontario College of Art in 1984. He graduated with honours from Humber College Arts Admin.

Other Books by Richard M. Grove

– "Beyond Fear and Anger" – Hidden Brook Press - 0-9699598-0-X

– "Poems For Jack" – Micro Prose – ISBN - 0-9699598-0-X

– "Trapped in Paradise" – Hidden Brook Press – ISBN 978-1-897475-57-7

– "Destination Cuba" – Hidden Brook Press – ISBN 978-1-927725-10-8

– "A View of Contrasts: Cuba Poems" – HMS Press – ISBN 1-894553-02-0

– "Sky Over Presqu'ile" – Hidden Brook Press – ISBN 1-894553-51-9

– "terra firma" – Hidden Brook Press – ISBN 978-1-894553-82-7

– "Oxido Rojo" – Hidden Brook Press – ISBN 978-1-894553-75-9

– "Substantiality" – Hidden Brook Press – ISBN 978-1-894553-74-2

– "The Family Reunion" – Hidden Brook Press – ISBN 978-1-894553-90-2

– "From Cross Hill" – Hidden Brook Press – ISBN 978-1-897475-15-7

– "Psycho Babble and the Consternations of Life"

    – Panegyric Press – ISBN 978-0-9732522-2-4

– "a trip to banes, cuba, 2002" – Hidden Brook Press – ISBN 978-1-897475-20-1

– "In This We Here the Light"– Hidden Brook Press – ISBN 978-1-897475-96-6

– "A Small Payback"– Hidden Brook Press – ISBN 978-1-927725-31-3

– "Two Thousand Seventeen"– SanBun Publishing – ISBN 978-93-84972-94-3

– "Living in the Shadow" – Hidden Brook Press – ISBN 978-1-927725-35-1

– "Some Sort of Normal" – Hidden Brook Press – ISBN 978-1-927725-63-4

– "The Importance of Good Roots"– Hidden Brook Press – ISBN 978-1-897475-97-3

www.ingramcontent.com/pod-product-compliance
Lightning Source LLC
Chambersburg PA
CBHW020544080526
44583CB00013B/993